OKANOGAN POEMS

Landscapes are Observatories

Grant Jones
Walter Henze
Editors

Coyote Springs Series
volume 3

Navajo Willow, Tunk Valley — Bob Goodwin

ISBN-13: 978-0-9796495-8-5

Copyright © 2016 by Skookumchuck Press
Grateful acknowledgement is extended to the authors of these poems for their permission to print.
All rights reserved. No part of this book may be used or reproduced in any manner whatsoever without written permission from the Publisher, except in the case of brief quotations embodied in critical articles and reviews.

Second Edition

Skookumchuck Press
Jones & Jones, 105 South Main Street #300, Seattle, Washington 98104
Publisher: Grant Richard Jones

Okanogan Poems
volume 3

Poets

George Baumgardner

Patti Baumgardner

Katharine Bill

Reed Engle

Bob Goodwin

Walter Henze

Dan Hulphers

Carey Hunter

Grant Jones

Victoria Jones

Mike Robinson

Roger Rosenblatt

William Slusher

Kathleen Smith

Dale Swedberg

Todd Thorn

Sandy Vaughn

Coyote Springs Series

This, the third volume of Okanogan Poems continues the tradition, established with the first two volumes, of celebrating hidden places in the watershed of the Okanogan River. It does that because the editor, Grant Jones, both a published poet and world renowned landscape architect, has come to this understanding with the wisdom of his years: by celebrating places we can influence their outcome.

The Okanogan Valley and its Eastern Highlands, a rural self sufficient region of high desert, lies in North Central Washingon, in Okanogan County – the largest county in Washington and one of the largest in the lower 48 states. The valley is well east of the Puget Sound megalopolis and the North Cascades. It is a magical place. Its west side is the upthrusted leading edge of the North Cascades Subcontinent, its east side is the trailing edge of Okanogan Subcontinent, and its valley bottom is all that is left of the seafloor between. This valley presents a spare and deceptively unassuming face to a traveler passing through along US Highway 97. That road follows the river's course, and the route of the old Cariboo Trail. I say deceptively unassuming because the topography of the valley floor presents a very limited shrub steppe viewshed. The higher elevations of this watershed, with spectacular mountains rising to over 8000 feet, high hidden valleys containing incredibly varied ecosystems, multiple tributary watersheds of rare beauty, these are all hidden from view if one simply sticks to the two lane blacktop thoroughfare. Such a traveler entirely misses the Tunk, the Chilliwist, the Siwash (Cho-Cho-We in the Native Salish language), the Antoine (pronounced ann-twyne), the Aeneas (the West Sanpoil), the Tonasket, the Sinlahekin, and Wild Horse Coulee – all scenic, extensive, long and beautiful valleys that drain into the Okanogan. Then there are the Okanogan Highlands (the southern end of the Canadian Monashees that terminate in Mount Bonaparte). From here, Meyers, the Toroda, the Curlew all drain eastward into the Kettle River and then on into the Columbia. In the appendix, we have included a complete listing of the watersheds and subwatersheds of this region.

These poems are a celebration of not only the land, but also the peoples of the region. As Grant said in the introduction to Volume 2, "All of these watersheds are alive with touchstone people: traditional native people of dozens of Native American tribes and First People bands, pioneer homesteaders, horse and cattle ranchers, enterprising town founders, fruit orchardists, vintners, organic farmers, carpenters, mountain hermits, poets, folk singers and those who just came to live on the land as landscape stewards. This place has not lost its stories nor its spirits and they keep evolving. It supports a rare, interconnected community of diverse people committed to hard work, cooperation, artistic expression and social tolerance."

The region includes most of the Confederated Tribes of the Colville Reservation, a group of 12 Native American tribes: Colville (Skoyelpi), Nespelem, Sandpoil (Sanpo-i-il), Lakes (Sinixt), Palus, Wenatchi, Chelan, Entiat (Wapato), Methow, Southern Okanogan (Sinkaietk), Moses Columbia (Sinkiuse) and Joseph Nez Perce. The entire region and more was the intrinsic homelands for thousands of years for these very diverse groups.

This entire area forms a major part of the area served by the Okanogan Land Trust. The OLT has been encouraging poetry of this place for seven years by hosting an annual Poetry Evening of readings by local poets. A number of the poems in this volume first appeared there. It is by celebrating places *out of sight and hence out of mind* that the poets here assembled give those places voice.

More recently, the region has been assaulted by catastrophic wild fires. In July and August of 2014, the Carlton Complex, then the largest fire in Washington State history, burned through almost 300,000 acres, in the Methow watershed. Then, this July, the Okanogan Complex consumed over 400,000 acres of the Okanogan, Kettle and Sanpoil Watersheds. Dale Swedberg's poem, *A Thirst Only Fire Can Quench,* which appears in Volume 2 of this series, addresses the effect that a century of fire suppression has had on creating the conditions that have led to these fires. In this Volume 3, Kathleen Smith's poem, *Dog Days of July*, and several of Bob Goodwin's *Okanogan Haikus 2015*, speak to what it is like to live through these fires.

WAH
Tamarack Farm
Pileated Creek Steward Catchment
North Burge Mountain
Lower Antoine Creek Sub Watershed
Okanogan River Sub Basin

Leaving's Becomings
in memory of Roger Rosenblatt

Our moment's memories
Fill my heart.
Mind's gardens
Grow through the seasons.
Your voice is in the trees.
Your cap's in my pocket.
Your footsteps scuff behind me.
Your knapsack's on my back
While we walk together talking.
Whose to say you ever left
When parting's becomings
Lead the way for
The love still growing.

GRJ
Coyote Springs Farm
Mouth of the Canyon of the Little Mosquito
Mosquito Creek-North Okanogan Mainstem Watershed
Okanogan River Sub Basin

Looking across Siwash to Whitestone   Bob Goodwin

Contents

George Baumgardner   11
    The Snow
    Snow Music Score
    Coyechoes

Patti Baumgardner   15
    Walk
    Bicycle
    Ski
    Home

Katharine Bill   21
    Storm
    What is Here?
    Radiate
    Winter Poem 1

Reed Engle   27
    The Swing Set

Bob Goodwin   29
    Okanogan Surf
    High Water
    Early Winters
    The Wauconda Barn
    Okanogan Haikus 2015

Walter Henze   37
    Gift from a Bobcat
    Growing Together
    The Clouds Over Arlington Ridge

Dan Hulphers   41
    Passing Clouds
    Rising Air
    Okanogan Highland Dreams

Carey Hunter   45
    My First Homestead
    Homestead #2
    Aspen Springs

Grant Jones   53
    Always There
    The Footbridge
    Open Thine Eyes--Talking to Beaverhead
    Northern Winter Solstice of 2014
    Braided River #2
    Two Coyote Tales: Bone Dreamers & Spirit Visitors
    Raptive Beauty
    The Backhoe Shed
    As Sociable and Loving as Handsome Wolves

Victoria Jones   71
    Poems from Aeneas Creek Canyon
    Poetry Can Be Heard
    Tanka Mama

Mike Robinson   75
    Observing a River

Roger Rosenblatt   79
    The Missing Okanogan Winter, 2014

William Slusher   81
    Not that Washington

Kathleen Smith   85
    How the Songs Come On Us
    Birdsong Blues
    Moth Wings
    Dog Days of July
    Will the Satellite Fall on Okanogan
    January

Dale Swedberg   93
    Sinlahekin - A Sense of Place

Todd Thorn   95
    Night in Coyote Canyon

Sandy Vaughn   97
    Highland Spring

George Baumgardner

Snow Music Score

Smooth
soft
scintillant snow
hieroglyph of snowshoe hare, quick-
stepped near by br'er coyote, seeking
a partner for his rhumba, that rhythmic
roundabout the forest
sings so true, by
night
and yes
by day.

Highlands Sno-Park
Upper Antoine Creek Sub Watershed
Okanogan River Sub Basin

The Snow

Yes, it's white,
but wait...

frost flakes flame
in rainbow bursts,
spectrum fractured filaments
flung far afield, while my
eyes with ripe delight
gather up these crystal glints
play fetch with them
till the night.

Henderson Steward Catchment
North Burge Mountain
Lower Antoine Creek Sub Watershed
Okanogan River Sub Basin

Coyechoes

last night, spelling myself between sauna times,
the quiet vibrated with autumnal resonance,
a clutch of coyotes graced the opportunity to harmonize withall,
tales of coyo-bravery and doggy foolishness, of spirit souls
lurching through sleepless nights
tethering with straining ears
those humans close enough in kind
to hear.

Henderson Steward Catchment
North Burge Mountain
Lower Antoine Creek Sub Watershed
Okanogan River Sub Basin

Patti Baumgardner

Walk

A giant snag, old and gnarled,
walks out of the white mist
and a great rock, rolled by ice
and dropped into place eons ago,
apparates from the fog, dripping lichen.

The forest pulses into space
left by trees gone to market,
long limbs loose,
gleaning droplets out of thin air.

Upper Spring Creek Steps Steward Catchment
North Burge Mountain
Lower Antoine Creek Sub Watershed
Okanogan River Sub Basin

Bicycle

Cycling toward Havillah from Sitzmark, the sky
is a big, fall blue with great streaks of white
flung across it, softening it.

Bonaparte stands to the east, its top catching
puffy swirls of cloud, its flank already
under snow along the Antoine.

In the roadside field,
the grain has been harvested and the short, yellow stubble reveals
drill lines, straight and narrow.

They roll to the west with the hill and the wheel
marks left by the tractor curve through them,
braiding them together.

At the top, Cascade peaks
line up between the field and the horizon, startlingly, like a crown
over the original cornrows.

Upper Antoine Creek Sub Watershed
Okanogan River Sub Basin

Ski

Now come the cold and the stillness.
Yet it's Solstice in the Highlands
and the morning snow is throwing huge sparks of light back to a
newly awakened sun.

Barely rolling across the ridge, our burning orb dissects surface
crystals into tiny prisms
that glitter the snow.

And in defiance of color,
a pair of ravens, dressed in black like we are,
fly in the blue, croaking Christmas bells.

Farther up the hill the sun backlights a twiggy deciduous tree full of
icicles, letting the branches emanate their own sparkling light.

If you ever find the artificial glow of this season
too glitzy, just go out and see what it is
that the sun, ice and snow do together.

Upper Antoine Creek Sub Watershed
Okanogan River Sub Basin

Home

Farmer friends tend
the tender greens that emerge from winter
torpor and cold, swollen spring.

They weed, prune, harrow, tie,
measure moisture, measure sugar,
wait for rain, wait for Okanogan sunshine.

They find tension with the climate, the weather,
the machines, the labor, the market.

Their brows grow as furrowed as their soil
but the day comes that is right to harvest
the perfect clusters, seed in bins, fruit in baskets, chaff blown to the
wind, vines unnetted for gleaning.

We gather, we crush, we grind, we culture
yeast and feed it Okanogan sugar.
We press, we beat, we fold, we rack,
we divide, we cool, we shape, we barrel,
we fire, we bottle and we wait hours or years.

Inconsequentially, time passes.

We peel the loaf off the hot oven stone.
It crackles. We set the bottle on the table.
It breathes. We sit with each other.
Each Day.
Sacred.
Okanogan. Communion.

Henderson Steward Catchment
Upper Antoine Creek Sub Watershed
Okanogan River Sub Basin

Wing Lake on Maple Pass — Katharine Bill

Katharine Bill

Storm

After hail quiet; frantic
energy released into
hardness, beating fists
upon spring's fickle ground; done.
Now.
Dissolving cold tension
with apologetic drizzle
the hard evidence remains; anger
at the lost love
the bittersweet air of almost.
Strained energy
released and
thawed;
could have fallen as gentle rain
on sweet spring beauties,
instead
force.
No ones fault,
just potential energy
accumulated over time
at once too much
and then gone.
Leaving mud on mountains
hammered and cold.

Washington Pass
Early Winters Sub Watershed
Methow River Sub Basin
14 April 2009

What is Here?

River here
smell of meltwater and silt
new to the world
current
fast.

Life here
vessel for experience
etching in
ceramic boundaries.

Edges here
of water on granite
of time on skin
    rough
of spirit on heart
    full and hot
    within arching sides
seductive boundaries
    uncertain ends.

Child's hand here
holding mine tight
we walk with purpose
to a flower
pull it off
pick it apart
throw it down
again.
and again.

Sunshine here
requires exposure
seeds require dirt
perhaps lost in soil
perhaps found in a child's hand.

River here
Life here
Spirit here.

Fawn Creek Sub Watershed
Methow River Sub Basin

Radiate

Colors of fall ending now
the late peak
fragile to the wind
falling leaves
one time only.

Dark up high
cold coming
time to put away
clean up
store.

Hello to what is next
open (patient, loving, strong?)
goodbye to green
now golden
grass
underneath
soon frozen
gone for this year; this year gone too;
one time only.

Fawn Creek Sub Watershed
Methow River Sub Basin

Winter Poem I

Inevitable transformation
sometimes catastrophic
release
sometimes incredible
plastic strength
water
sculpted
translucent.
Why worry when this blanket
covers regularity
with the miracle of water
why not enjoy the sanctity
safety
silence?

Fawn Creek Sub Watershed
Methow River Sub Basin

Reed Engle

The Swing Set

I'm busy now building, a swing set
Eleven feet tall in this heat by myself.
Not so fast, but care fully
(To avoid mishap and potential injury)
Challenged both physically and mentally I remind
Myself not to hurry about this, three braces staked
At grade with an allowance for a pivot, ready now
Tools at hand, the hundred and seventy pound post
Is guided from the elevated lumber rack
Into the thirty-six inch hole and righted in the air
Eleven feet vertical and slowly, methodically
Braced, plumb to the Earth and sky--
Challenging alone,
But, What fun!

The Saddle, Homestead Ridge
Middle Antwyne Canyon
Lower Antoine Creek Sub Watershed
Okanogan River Sub Basin
7 June 2015

Bob Goodwin

Okanogan Surf

Out past Hess Lake, Barnett Bluff
records in its limestone mass
ancient earth's convulsions,
frozen in serpentine folds.
How so in brittle ocean rock?
Can you hear the surf?
Can you smell the wrack?

Limebelt Road, Cave Mountain,
names that speak of warm seas
bordering island continents,
sailing on magma rafts,
to dock against our shores.
Can you hear the surf?
Can you smell the wrack?

Not one smooth slide, but
trains of lurching temblors
raised our mountains foot by foot,
and loosed great tides to sweep strange
creatures from their coastal plains.
Can you hear the surf?
Can you smell the wrack?

Our Okanogan Vale,
a geologic seam,
stitching fast two continents,
mating fossilized shores,
their waves forever stilled.
Can you hear the surf?
Can you smell the wrack?

Hess Lake and Barnett Bluff
Johnson Creek Sub Watershed
Okanogan River Sub Basin

High Water

High in the Pasayten
last winter's snow
kissed by a late spring sun
shape-shifts itself to water,
trickles to join other storms'
snow-melt to feed a creek,
then another, swelling in time
to a bank-full stream.

Pasayten joins Similkameen
tumbles over falls, then
hesitates on the flats
by Nighthawk, unsure
which way gravity pulls.

Wouldn't do to confuse
the naming geographers
by spilling into Palmer Lake
and thence the Sinlahekin
(Similkameenlahekin?)

Meandering slowly east
to pick up speed down the
doomed wild reach above
damned Enloe dam,
Similkameen rushes by
its confluence with
lesser sibling Okanogan.

On the flood, brown as chocolate,
trees, branches, stumps with
root-balls snatched from perches
safe since last high water,
slide with the current past
Valley towns to founder
like beached whales on the flats

where the Okanogan adds
its color to the Columbia.

Before the main stem dams
Changed river to settling ponds,
Pasayten sand built beaches
on the Cascadian Coast.

Now winter storms demanding
tribute, sever spits, cut into bluffs.
The sea reclaims the land
the river can't sustain.

Think on this as turbines spin
to charge your phones and
burn your morning toast.

Palmer Lake and Creek Sub Watershed
Similkameen River Sub Basin

Early Winters

"Thanksgiving is yet a week off
But frost feathers needles on the firs
The sycamore still sheds leaves
To litter the fresh fallen snow.
Is this distemperature from Titania's pique?
Are these hoary-headed frosts of
Oberon's making?
If so, let them soon make up before our planet burns
After an early winter's freezing."

Omak Sand Flat
Swipkin Creek-Okanogan River Reach
Okanogan River Sub Basin

The Wauconda Barn

The old barn is gone from the High Country
near the limestone quarry past Wauconda Grange.
Not a trace remains in the meadow it graced
for over a hundred saddle ranching years.

Architecture without artifice, the Western Barn
is an endangered species, an unpretentious form
shaped by necessities: high in the center
with large paired doors for wagons;
low at the sides for pony stalls,
ridge extended to lift grain
by a hook into the hay loft,
stockaded by split rail pens and chutes.

Slowly bent by winter snows
its ridge yields to gravity's pull.
An ATV can replace a horse,
no one cares enough to fix
a loose board, leaks in the roof.
Walls bow, nails pop;
then, last Spring, with creaks
and groans that were heard by a pair of ravens,
marmots, perhaps a passing coyote,
the old barn folds itself into the meadow.

It's rough sawn boards were scavenged in a day
by city folk in glossy trucks
to clad their recroom walls,
lichens lodged still in the grain,
patinas no stain could ever match,
bagged and displayed like wild trophies.

Grasses in the meadow keen a soft lament
Barn swallows swoop back and forth to search
out last summer's nests. A barn owl,
seeks sanctuary but finds no roost.

The old barn is gone from the High Country
near the limestone quarry past Wauconda Grange.
Will it fade from that meadow's memory?
I must mark it with a split rail poem.

Toroda Creek Sub Watershed
Okanogan River Sub Basin
January 2015

Okanogan Haikus 2015

Green mists rise with sap,
Winter boughs' stark lines grow soft:
Hopes of early Spring.

The horse's shadow
longer than the two acre field:
Dawns a summer day.

Nighthawks whirr and dive
insecticidal sorties:
Summer sun setting.

Winds howl a red night
rolling over tinder woods:
Blackened moonscape dawn.

Slanting early light
scraping darkness off charred hills:
Bright ellipse of hope.

Omak Sand Flat looking across the river to Wanacut Creek Watershed
Swipkin Creek-Okanogan River Reach
Okanogan River Sub Basin

Walter Henze

Gift from a Bobcat

Hiking Burge Mountain, on a sharp winter morning,
My path cut the track of a Bobcat;
A track in snow that had ended at midnight,
A track fresh by hours, perhaps even minutes.

I altered my course and I followed.

He contoured the mountain, through timber and thicket,
And we became bound by the thread he unspooled,
Cat, mountain and I, conjoined.

As I gathered that thread I could picture his movements.
Here slower, here faster, here vaulting the downfalls,
His prints neatly paired on the tops of the logs.

Then his track started curving, winding up a small knob
Where he sat and surveyed before changing his way
To drop down a ravine tightly packed with debris,
So steep and so dense, was no route for me.

Had he sauntered last night, heading home to his den?
Or vanished just now, as I entered his ken.

I turned back onto the ridge, breaking our thread.
Warmed to the core by our brief dance together,

Smiling out loud at the gift of his presence.

Burge Mountain
Stagecoach Spring Steward Catchment
Lower Antoine Creek Sub Watershed
Okanogan River Sub Basin

Growing Together

Over 40 years ago, more than half my life ago,
A new friend pulled me from Seattle
Out to the Okanogan
With the promise of sunshine and heat.

And women and beer.

We worked together with other new friends
To raise the rafters on his hand built log cabin,
    Massive and imposing.

Ok, well, twelve by sixteen feet, to be precise.

And so it was not long thereafter, I moved to the Okanogan.
Over the years and the decades that cabin grew, and our families grew,

And we grew older together.

And though my friend, alas, is no longer with us,
His soul remains.
He's easy to find
Among the pines on the Little Loup.

We talk together, he and I, about the forest and the trees, and our families,

All growing, strong and tall.

Little Loup Loup Creek Sub Watershed
Okanogan River Sub Basin

Dan Hulphers

Passing Clouds

Passing clouds cast shadows
rolling darkly
over green highland hills
strewn with wild flowers
whose brilliance fades
until the cloud passes
then burst forth brightly
until the next dark caress

Mary Ann Creek Sub Watershed
Kettle River Sub Basin

Rising Air

A hillside of tall grass flows in waves
inscribing a breeze
aspens shimmer and rustle
reaching into the wind
a hawk floats higher and higher
on uplifting air
the streaked sky
streams inexorably north
these poignant atmospheric vicissitudes
of the invisible

Mary Ann Creek Sub Watershed
Kettle River Sub Basin

Okanogan Highland Dreams
(to be sung with guitar)

At last alone on a midnight hill
a clever breeze whispers secrets in the pines
on the dark cloth of night a cosmic sugar spill
a broken moon stumbles over the power lines

(chorus)   and here we are, unlikely as it seems
            beneath our lucky star
            these Okanogan highland dreams

A coyote's aria, an owl hoots and takes flight
a big rig rumbles over the pass
this brief theater, an opera of the night
then it's gone with a gust through the tall summer grass

(chorus repeat)

Lady Bug Mountain
Baker Creek Sub Watershed
Kettle River Sub Basin

The Clouds Over Arlington Ridge

Below Arlington Ridge, my friend gone now a dozen
Months or more, lies in last repose.
He lay beneath green pines, until lightning
Cracked the air on Beaver Creek and changed the land forever.

Now, the forest he nurtured so heartfully is gone,
The house he built so carefully is gone,
The cabin we raised so joyfully is gone,

All so suddenly ashes to ashes.

His ashes lie neath the charred spar of his favored tree,
Beneath a blanket of forest ash spread over the land for miles.
He pledged he would return as a larch on the turn of the wheel.
A seed stirring beneath the ash, beneath the snow, will be that tree.

I visit this bare and open place that's waiting for traces of green
    and promise,
But rocks and the ridge and the sky are all that remain.

In the heat of the sun, this blackened land breathes out,
It's warmed breath rising, bearing aloft its nano bits of ash.

Ashes to ashes, ashes to air,
The nidus, seed, for the clouds that form in the sky
    over Arlington Ridge.

Little Loup Loup Creek Sub Watershed
Okanogan River Sub Basin

Carey Hunter

My First Homestead

Hiked in on New Year's Day
1971.
Snow was knee deep,
Hills rolled gently upward,
Warming me with the climb.
Cresting the rise, before us
A hip-roofed house,
Faded yellow, nestled in a meadow
Ponderosas in a receding hairline,
Curved round to frame the scene.
Pristine
and yet
Already someone had come
In 1902 and built
This house, come to find out.

We borrowed $500
And for $50 a month
This dream became ours to work.
Sweet, back-busting work,
Decades of packrat condos
Cleaned and packed out.
First long summer spent camping
Au plein air.
Okanogan sunshine,
Fresh air and quiet spaces
Seduced our willing spirits.
By Fall in a cozy house
We burned our last chair leg.
As we walked out and looked West
Over waves of colliding plates
We felt our place in a landscape
That beached itself here eons before

The vision kept us strong
In our retreat to civilization for the winter
Laboring for a homestead vision,
Now a burgeoning reality.

Barker Mountain
Siwash Creek Watershed
Okanogan River Sub Basin

View West on road to Barker Mountain   Carey Hunter

Homestead #2

Eighteen years after my first essay,
I found what I was looking for.
"Low Expectations," I called it,
Afraid to get my hopes up.

Nameless. It was up for back-taxes auction,
Abandoned & derelict,
Pipes...frozen & burst,
Detritis from a series of derelict inhabitants.

But the location, aah, the location grabbed,
Close enuf yet far enuf.
Sweet-scented Pine trees again,
Wind thru their branches.

It felt to my landlubber's ears like the ocean.
Not so remote,
But still miles past other houses.
Eager to leave town's constricting confines,

I leapt at the opportunity, liberated into the woods.
Camping au plein
Air again, the ocean
In the Pine branches filled me, settled me.

Breathing deep, listening out.
I cast a blanket
And laid down in the sounds and sensations,
Waiting to exhale, listening out –

Once again in the woods again.

Pine Stump Farm
French Valley
Omak Creek Sub Watershed
Okanogan River Sub Basin

Aspen Springs

I happened upon it
When the scorched dry of
Late August and
The Fires had ravaged us.
Searching for a bit of respite
And solace
Instinctively knowing
Knowing where to look for the springs.
So I readied the horse and took off
South by a bit southwest.
Remembering a curve of the trail
That led to a dip in the gulley
And tracing that downhill
I found the spring
Tucked into a crevice of the hill
Seeping out to a gentle slope.
Verdant moss had retained its color;
Cradled by old logs.
I sighed and breathed deep.

Looking up and across the gulley
I saw the landscape with refreshed eyes.
Knowing that time would heal,
Changing the scorched terrain.
The surviving green sentinels announce
The faith and optimism they hold
Across a lifespan longer than mine.
My mare wants to move on,
So I urge her forward .
Upwards, around the precious spring
That shared its secret being with me
And gifted me with reassurance.
I had secured a glimpse of what I was seeking.

The remainder of the ride was couched in that success
And the damaged trees & earth
Didn't seem so desolate.

Each day now
I think back to that ride and its gifts:
My trusty mare, the precious spring, the
sentinel trees, the glorious sunshine
Breathe deep again
And shoulder on.

Pine Stump Farm
French Valley
Omak Creek Sub Watershed
Okanogan River Sub Basin

Grant Jones

Always There

The sun has climbed up
behind Pack Pony Hill
coursing along a couple hundred feet
above the sage and greasewood.
Chong just hung out the laundry
on the line. If this keeps up
they'll be smelling of ozone
when we get back from the post office.
It's 12 degrees.
We named the ridge behind the house
Watch Over Us Hill:
metamorphic rocks stand
in a family up there
catch the sun and smile
on us with their good spirits.
Of course they're always there.

Written at Coyote Springs Farm,
Mouth of the Little Mosquito Creek-Okanogan Sub Watershed,
Okanogan River Sub Basin, Columbia River Basin
December 7, 2014

The Footbridge

The footbridge connects the house to the barn.
Sitting on it now my feet,
Like ducks in my creek,
Connect me to the North Pacific's spinning gyre
Like a battery that turns the world.
It changes my tide four times a day.
Last night's moon lifted fresh coconuts
Out of Wailua River on Kauai Island
And scattered them up Lumahai Beach to shade the lovers.
I'm reborn every time I go to the barn.

Written at Coyote Springs Farm,
Little Mosquito Creek-Okanogan Sub Watershed,
Okanogan River Sub Basin, Columbia River Basin
March 22, 2014

Beaverhead Glowing   Chong Jones

Open Thine Eyes: Talking to Beaverhead

You are not alone
This moment
It waits
Until your awake
It's always there
But where have you been?

And here you are
Part of everything
But changed
Transformed
Searching
Then where'd it go?

There is no other
It won't come here again
It's everywhere
It's the space between
But don't call it nothing
Because it's everything.

It's watching
It's listening
It's holding you up
It's lifting you
It pulls you on
It's gravity itself.

It's in your heart
It's inside you head
It's a spirit
It's you
It's me
There is no other.

It's not the future
It's not the past
It's before
It's beyond
It's now
Is that all there is to it?

It's in your eyes
In your hair
In your fingers
All across your skin
And it pulses in your hands
And in theirs--your friends and lovers.

It's in your breath
It makes words come out of nowhere
It remembers everything
It remembers me
It remembers you
It gives you a voice.

It forgets nothing
It's all around you
But you can't own it
It waits
It feels your feelings
Are you connected?

Why do you wonder so?
Why do you struggle?
Why are you lost?
Why do you feel guilty?
Where do get the idea you've sinned?
Nothing is wrong. Open your eyes.

Respect your Mountain's presence
It remembers your love
Shine out yourself so it can see you
Feels its breath when it cools you in the evening
It's heart pounds strongest if you open your eyes.
Give it a nod before turning in...
"Sleep Well, Mountain!"

"Good Morning," Mountain of my dreams.
"You're lookin' good, better than you should"...
Considering what you know by now
Of the general state of human affairs,
From Aeneas to Anchorage and from Antwyne to Albuquerque,
Let alone from Astoria to Ankkor Wat,
Or Alderwood Manor to Amboseli or, you know what I mean--
And we're still in the first letter of the alphabet.

But the creek keeps chuckling with gifts from your springs,
Colder and clearer each year you've been watching us;
And the snowflakes this morning swirling off your brow
Gather and braid up like the Cottonwood seeds
Make drifts along our road to the barn each spring,
Or the way Chokecherries blow blossoms on our pond like brush strokes.
That's how you talk back to us, and why I reply with this poem.
"Thanks, Beaverhead!"

Coyote Springs Farm
Little Mosquito Creek Canyon
Mosquito Creek-Okanogan Sub Watershed
Okanogan River Sub Basin

Northern Winter Solstice of 2014

Humans marked
This moment over hundreds of thousands of years,
A turning point:
Shortest day and longest night
Northern Hemisphere.

Owls, jays, juncos, coyotes,
Wolverines and bison
Have known for a million years
Our sun is lowest on the horizon today
And will be stalled here over a week.
If you want to watch sunrises and sunsets you'll see.
You could smile, now: We're heading toward Spring!
Or you could frown today: It's the beginning of Winter!

A day to be one with your light
In the perfect continuum of a year on Earth,
The day to put up the fence along O'Neil Road
At Coyote Springs Farm on the mouth of the Little Mosquito.

Coyote Springs Farm
Mouth of the Canyon of the Little Mosquito
Okanogan River Sub Basin

sol=sun, sistere=to stand stationary; the sun stalls for 12 days=Yule fires Celts have celebrated for 50,000 years to insure rebirth of the sun;
The Jewish Talmud has celebrated since the 1st c. the sun's return 8 days before and 8 days after the northern winter solstice.
The Catholic Church in the 3rd century overlays the birth of Christ, the Son of God.

Braided River #2

Maybe if I'd kept on going to that big doctor in Seattle,
I would have died a long time ago. But lifting
the pitcher pump handle seven times
lifts a gallon of water cold and clear
and sweet from twelve feet down the hand-dug
homestead well to bring inside
before we eat four apples from our tree
each morning with the handground coffee just before
I shave and brush my teeth
before we feast on the radishes and onions, tomatoes
and peppers we brought in for Chong's strong hand's
to chop into the magic of her Coho kimchi
now bursting in my mouth like the Nesbitt's orange pop
I liked as a kid,
That I'm still here so glad to be alive.

Coyote Springs Farm
Mouth of the Canyon of the Little Mosquito
Okanogan River Sub Basin
October 4, 2014

Two Coyote Tales

Bone Dreamer
in memory of Bob MacDill, cowboy poet

I lived among Coyotes at the mouth of the canyon.
I still wear the young pup's collarbone I found in the creek.
I heard his kettling, falsetto yipping.
But it's his spirit to play, in the stars, that I keep.
I used to be as quick as a ferret, but now
I'm so still the Flickers buzzbomb my hair
When I lean on a fencepost and go

Poó, yip poó, yip poó,
Poodi hoó, di yip poó, di yip poó,
Poó, yip poó, yip poó,
Poodi hoó, di yip poó, di yip poó.

Spirit Visitors

They passed behind the broken tree,
the walnut shaking in the wind.
One moved hunched on four legs
low in grass dried out brown
color of dirt. The other fluttered,
followed smaller like a tumble weed,
catching up and falling behind.

It jerked dust and belly slithered,
and trailed the leader stalking his shadows.
Shadows? or were they shifts in afterlight?
Well that's what I saw I guess, shadows.
But then the big one's eyes burned my Filson
tin-vest, cooked its paraffin
sweet enough to eat.

Coyote Springs Farm
Mouth of the Canyon of the Little Mosquito
Okanogan River-Mosquito Creek Watershed
Okanogan River Sub Basin

Raptive Beauty

Hawks are not social.
They are singleminded
looking for kills to eat.
All hawks aren't successful.
My "raptive beauty" is elegant,
beautifully put together with
no evidence of wrecks
marring its perfect plumage.
He or she must be pretty
successful in gyrating, spinning
high-speed, blasting through branches full-tilt.
This gymnastic beauty stalks
a cross section of little birds,
some easier, some difficult to nab
from their perches, suggesting
acquired preferences
for certain prey, but with skill
to handle a diversity of kills
some delicious with few feathers,
some all bony inside deep feathered
hairballs. The skill is in the tail,
but the meat of some tastes better,
is easier to defeather, so my hawk
plays his or her options not
from hunger but for the delight
of pleasurable outcomes.

You're meditating on a lichened fence post,
rotating your head with its sexy,
wind-ruffed crown, your coffee-brown pupils
flaming peacefully in their blood-pink irises.

The slate-blue maxilla of your beak
arcs like a linoleum knife
from its moss-green nasal tufts,
the dark nostril holes like compass points.

Your muscular neck, foamy-cream nape and throat,
is bulging warm against the wind;
your cape of cobalt-gray scapulars floating from its mantle,
while your wings nestle like bow scythes.

When you're ready you'll corkscrew through the serviceberries
pick off a few puffs of passerine protein,
steered by that swiveling triple-black tail rudder,
perfect for the yaw, pitch, and roll of your acquired tastes.

Inspired by my sighting and Art Campbell's Cooper's Hawk photographs posted on ncwabird.
Coyote Springs Farm
Mouth of the Canyon of the Little Mosquito
Okanogan River-Mosquito Creek Watershed
Okanogan River Sub Basin

The Backhoe Shed

It's been good for my soul
Working with Reed,
Talking to the birch tree
Measuring for its flexations with the rafters
Staking the batter boards
Picking through the old posts and boards
From our recycle stack behind the barn,
Setting the pier boxes
Shooting the grades
Tightening up the stringlines
And centering the roach clips.
Mixing the mud
Pouring and placing the postbrackets
And screeding them off;

Waiting while they set-up overnight
Then stripping the forms,
Hearing a few songs
From the Bitterroot commune
Frosty Creek melodies
Brought down to the Eel and back again
To the skylines of the Antwyne…
Hearing Reed's homestead stories.

Yesterday my neighbor Bob,
Up the canyon on Wizard's Flat,
Shoveled, screened and loaded
Four yards of Beaverhead shale
In his International dumptruck
Piling it off our driveway
So I can spread it with the Kubota backhoe
Dressing out the floor of the new Pickup Shed
Edged now with five ancient four-by-fours
We got from Phil at Havillah Shake
Wood yard and sawmill down 97
Toward the Janis Rapids

Saving my countless ass
In every mutation we've triggered
Like when the barn collapsed
Or the house needed mutating,
Like when the tractor shed flooded
And the creek washed the road out,
Or when we needed the Camp Kitchen
To have a tall, hovering Tapanco roof,
Wanted a woodshed for a four-cord winter,
A deerfence around the vegetables,
Or portal gates to the Riverbraids Garden,
Beams for a footbridge to harbor our *minari*
The water celery that coils in our kimchi
Or posts to tie the moon
And keep the coyotes yipping
For any number of reasons
That keep the Earth in one piece.

Coyote Springs at the Mouth of the Little Mosquito
Mosquito Creek-North Okanogan Sub Watershed
Okanogan River Sub Basin
June 6, 2015

Whitestone Knuckles — Grant Jones

As Sociable and Loving as Handsome Wolves

We crossed the river after dawn
as a fresh breeze from the north
blew the oily scent of lambs
off Whitestone Mountain's hip.

Leaves from the poplars had backfilled
the fence where seven lambs waited through the night.

Trailrunner George and mate Patti
broke the ridge first with Rendezvous Donal
followed by Teacher Scott.
Ranchfather Tom stood still by a tall poplar.
Shaman Grant and Healer Chong trailed in behind.
We came to slaughter seven lambs,
as sociable and loving as handsome wolves.

Shadows of morning banded Whitestone's knuckles
as we closed in circling the lambs.
George rolled the first to the ground and made
his end-of-the-trail mortise while Patti held down
and gentled the lamb, leaving its last breaths
to the wind in our hair under the tall poplars.

None of this could have happened without Ranchmother Linda's
energizing breakfast and lunch for the pack.

Black's Bench
Whitestone Mountain-Horse Springs Coulee Watershed
Okanogan River Sub Basin
October 17, 2015

Tipi frame   Victoria Jones

Victoria Jones

Poems from Aeneas Creek Canyon

White top and redroot
Took over the bank.
Chlorophyl green, rampant and rank.
In bud and in bloom
Their weedy hearts sank
As a gardener came and
Gave them a yank!

We chanced to look up---
A perfect V of snow geese
Silent, dazzling
Cuts a wake in cold air waves.
Half a milky moon glimmers.

Bee's friend is blooming
Scorpioid inflorescence
Apian confab
Lavender clouds unfurling
Pollen politics takes wing.

A vulture's shadow
Dark green on a golden slope
Skims through tall grasses.

Blue Heron at dusk
Dark silhouette on night sky
Stitching up the stars
Look up----a shooting star!
As it burns I wish for wings.

Spinning gold from straw
My life's fibers are weaving
A rich tapestry.

Indian Springs Steward Catchment, Aeneas Creek Canyon
Aeneas Creek Sub Watershed, Okanogan River Sub Basin

Poetry Can Be Heard

Poetry can be heard
In the silent wish
When a golden comet streaks the night sky
Connecting the star dots.
It is the lullaby
The waterfall whispers
To the mossy rocks.

Poetry is the scent
Of new mown hay and rank weeds
Wafting in my cabin window-----
Drifting like a sleepwalker in the dimness.
It is the purple whiff of lavender
Tucked in my pillowcase...
The promise of dreams.

Poetry can be felt
In the friction of flannel sheets
And the featherweight of a down comforter
As autumn begins.
It is body heat captured under quilts.

Poetry is sensed
In the invisible movement
Of a creature silently shadowing about
In the darkness.

In the morning light
I see a message printed on my deck
In sloppy brown script.
In her slender paw prints beaver wrote
A secret mud poem.

Indian Springs Steward Catchment, Aeneas Creek Canyon
Aeneas Creek Sub Watershed, Okanogan River Sub Basin

Tanka Mama

Listen to the hawks
Fill up your space with freedom
Exalt in stretched wings
Newly fledged and shimmering
Trust invisible updrafts

Like cupid's arrow
Twenty six geese shoot eastward
Hearts are a-quiver.
Flocking, banding and pairing
Sticking out their necks for love.

Magpies pick the bones
Sacrificial venison
Torpor of winter.

Indian Springs Steward Catchment
Aeneas Creek Canyon
Aeneas Creek Sub Watershed
Okanogan River Sub Basin

Mike Robinson

Observing A River
(homage to *Methow Naturalist* editor Dana Visalli)

How you got here was nothing
like water. (When Greek gods fell,
they fell heavy as fullbacks
enchanted by cheerleaders,
loose tunics draped over wet stone.)

That seam between two slicks
hints at a fish...but eye it, see
how its riffle fades,
infatuation wandering, quick as whims.

Don't move that way
unless you want wonder:
sunrise that splits you,
gravel gathering in your mouth.

What drinks here waits all night,
after the deer bed down, after
shadows extend wide wings,
after moonlight washes
topwater paler than a moth.

It's almost enough to make
a fisherman hold still hip deep,
lay down his life, step
all the way in. You know
that urge, your favorite lure?

It was not on your map,
it ran like water in your veins.
You hear its tick, lying awake
at three, its muddy signal
clear as a creek, calling you home.

Lower Middle Methow River Sub Watershed
Middle Methow River Watershed
Methow River Sub Basin
Okanogan Basin

Roger Rosenblatt

The Missing Okanogan Winter of 2014

If snowflakes are hexagonal
Why aren't they more plentiful?
Their skeletons so symmetrical
They slide 'neath our skis.

And where were these creatures
With their crystalline features
When we began to have seizures
At the absence of snow?

In seasons predictable
In the cadence meteorological
We would swath our chins' follicles
With scarves and with skins

And those near the Loup
Would ordinarily swoop
In a disorderly troop
To the lodge far below.

But bad poetry can't change the fate
That the snow that drew us here
To this far corner of this corner state
Will soon disappear;

And though prosaic and grim
Unless we begin
To acknowledge our sin,

We will be remembered
As those who dismembered
The world we were in.

Little Loup Loup Creek, Arlington Ridge
Loup Loup Creek Sub Watershed, Okanogan River Sub Basin

William Slusher

Not That Washington

Washington!, they cry ... all rain ... and snow! Why wish would anyone there to go?

Washingtonians ... crazy they, who never do know an unfoggy day.

Whales and airliners and a rocky coast, of precious little more can Washington boast.

Why go you there, they ask of me, why leave our ... lovely ... civilized ... East?

****

But not to that Washington do I go, I protest, that Washington was never to be my quest ...

no ... I go to the little known central high-lands, the rolling, desert, sagebrush, dry lands.

I go where the salt always shakes, the sugar always pours, where the wind blows dry and the waterfalls roar.

I go where nothing rots and nothing rusts, where there're moose in the roads and the cowboys cuss.

I go where the eagle dives, and the cougar stalks, where the Indians dance and the Sasquatch walks!

I go under the glorious Northern Lights, where the stars are laser in the cold black nights ...

... where seasons are four and well defined, where old dreamers seek gold in the canyons to mine.

****

I go to the highlands that shake with quakes, where February freezes and August bakes.

In summer the Fire Beast rises to rage, hot, angry and hungry, and scorching the sage.

In winter, avalanches close highways, in the spring wildflowers color byways.

I go where mountains slide, where Native drums thump, where wolves hide and the nights go bump,

I go where fighter jets soar, their pilots to train, where the rancher wonders is it ever gonna rain?

There're more square miles than people out there, freeways and subdivisions are rare.

No, it's out to the high-land desert I go, it's farrrr from the Washington you think you know.

****

The highlands aren't a place you can learn from books, they take much more than a distant look.

You have to feel the heat and smell the smoke, and slip on the ice where bones get broke ...

... you must drive the tractors and ride the horses, you must track the creeks all the way to their sources.

You must weep from the windblown dust in your eyes, you must hear in the darkness the coyote cries.

You must love roads, empty, far out of sight. You must ... tremble ... when the sky glows orange in the night!

****

Noooo ... you stay here in your ... East of ... fame. I've seen it and I'll pass, thanks just the same.

I like to drive for an hour and see two cars, where the Big Dipper shines and so does Mars ...

... where women blow snot feeding cows before dawn, where out your kitchen window there may lie a fawn,

where distant Cascades make your spirits lift, where our kids get guns for baby shower gifts.

****

Noooo ... you stay here in the East. You won't like it out there, you'll just lose sleep and stay all scared,

The highlands are not the place for thee, no ... you stay here ... and leave the West to me.

Buttercup Falls
McLoughlin Reach Okanogan River
Between the mouth of Chewiliken Creek and the Tunk
March 7, 2015

Kathleen Smith

How the Songs Come On Us

After dinner we two sit by the fire
in the cabin, sipping good wine,
the old dog snoring at our feet.
Tonight coyote songs float through
the valley, their cadenced chorus
gliding like fog, over rounded hills.
As the circle tightens, the dog
lifts his wolfen head and sniffs.
We pause, go out for wood;
know later might be out of rhythm,
too little or too late. The air thickens
with our listening: we three
soft animals straining to guage
the distance between song and selves.

The dog stands up and howls.
Both songs rise around our ears,
raise hair on arms and necks.
A question catches in our throats.
We know there's hunger in this song.
Is it a feast song for our fire,
or are we the feast tonight?
Outside blurry shapes lurk
in shadow just beyond the cabin's
safe arc of firelight. The coyotes howl,
hurl wild metaphors against the night,
still hunger for more meat, more song.
Songs are circling, circling close.
Some metaphors can bite.

East Molson Hill
Mary Ann Creek Sub Watershed, Kettle River Sub Basin

Birdsong Blues

Often in poems a bird perches
on a bough and sings or takes flight,
making poetic hearts soar.
More often our headlights
frame a great grey owl gorging
his bloody dinner on a mountain road.
At noon on that same dry road
two magpies freeze a snake
and strip it to bones in ten minutes.
A young dog scavenges through roadside
brush and struts out with the entire front leg
of a fawn, the table scrap of golden eagles.
Far more honest to mention birds like raven
and the albatross. But sudden death
haunts birds as well: that raucous blue
jay now crying softly as raccoons plunder
her nest; a murder of crows murmuring
at the funeral of the young one who fell.
Raven got the blues and stole the sun.
You know the stories. Listen to their songs.

East Molson Hill
Mary Ann Creek Sub Watershed
Kettle River Sub Basin

Moth Wings

Every winter the cabin stands quiet and cold,
snow on the roads too deep to clear for human
solitude. Some heat seeps in from low sun
dropping early behind the hilly aspen grove.
Warmth and protein are scarce. At night, the glow
of moon on snow shows, that even here, the carnage
of the world goes on. Mice, whose blood is warm
and pumped by small and shivering hearts, catch
cold-blooded moths made sluggish in this season.
Every spring we find their wings piled in cabin corners,
their soft silver wings scorned by carnivores,
good for nothing except fair weather flight.
Poets, who stretch to reach the wings of poems
flying by, do well to watch and learn
the patience of a single starving mouse.

Easy Molson Hill
Mary Ann Creek Sub Watershed
Kettle River Sub Basin

Dog Days of July

The big fire in the Methow hangs its smokey umbrella over my sun.
All day it has been twilight.All day the fire, just one range over, weighs us down.
It's like turning on the radio and getting Mideast body count when all you really
wanted
was old blues. Death's not right here, but its close air hovers. The more sensitive
among
us
choke
up
more
easily.
When
I
was
young
I
was
tough.
Now
I
catch
myself
catching
my breath.

Omak West Bank Bluff
Okanogan River-Swipkin Canyon Reach
Okanogan River Sub Basin

Will the Satellite Fall on Okanogan?

I think of all that expensive junk
splashing into the river that divides
the cowboys from the Indians up here.
Folks who came here to flee the space race,
rat race and tech race waking, sipping
coffee by their woodstoves,

and hearing that great splash.
Shocking how all the worlds lie under just one sky.

Omak West Bank Bluff
Okanogan River-Swipkin Canyon Reach
Okanogan River Sub Basin

January

Listen to Patsy Cline
as the geese settle on the river.
Taste the sweetness of sorrow,
the goodness of downtime.
For this, we cherish
fog and whiskey,
winter and nightfall.

Tomorrow light the fire
and set the table. Tomorrow
take a bath and cook.
Tonight is for wallowing,
settling in like the geese
into deep and silent eddies,
watching your breath rise
like the steam on the river.

Omak West Bank Bluff
Okanogan River-Swipkin Canyon Reach
Okanogan River Sub Basin

Dale Swedberg

Sinlahekin - A Sense of Place

Belong to the land
I want to be
I search for
What does it mean
I belong to the land
A sense of place

To understand
To belong to the land
More knowledge I seek
Insatiable yearning makes me weak
I belong to the land
A sense of place

To know
Fauna and Flora
Who they are
What they do
How we fit
I belong to the land
A sense of place

To understand
Processes biotic and abiotic
Past and present
How they create today
I belong to the land
A sense of place

Sinlahekin Creek Sub Watershed
Similkameen River Sub Basin

Todd Thorn

Night in Coyote Canyon

Coyote Canyon at night,
Quiet and still save for lonely travelers driving through,

When the moon is big, the towering canyon walls gleam
And seem to lean in high above the road;
During winter storms, the bedrock rim drags snow from low cold clouds,
Muffling road noise from a few cars;
Other nights a spark of light from ten thousand stars
Illuminates this narrow, wild space of boulders and trees,
A small stream collects along the dark canyon floor,
Source of Coyote Creek.

In the dark, a tiptoeing moose might dip its head and sip from the little pond nestled below the summit,
Not even ruffling two dozing teal;
Bear would traverse this chasm, just passing through along its continual forest sojourn.
But Bigfoot is always present, maybe just a sculpture
Or spirit being
Waiting for acknowledgement,
A simple nod of respect from passers-by will do.

Coyote Creek Sub Watershed
Hopkins Canyon Reach of the Columbia River Sub Basin

Sandy Vaughn

Highland Spring

Ah, the relentless nature of Spring...inexorable,
   It will come...still every year we hold our collective breath.

Cynics we may well be in worldly affairs
But yet hopeful at heart we wonder,
   Will Spring really come again, and all at once?
Or in bits of blooms, and nips at winter's icy hand.

Now, grey wet wild wind, brown hills,
   Flattened grasses just relieved from the burden of snow.

Then sunlit shaft, and fragrance of warm soil.

Meyers Creek Sub Watershed
Kettle River Sub Basin

Places

Hidden Valleys of the Okanogan Country

This is the third volume in this series published to celebrate the nature of the American Okanogan and to give a voice to its scenic landscapes seen through the eyes of poets that inhabit or regularly explore the hidden valleys of this sequestered region.

In the Similkameen: Palmer Lake, Upper Sinlahekin Creek, Lower North Fork Touts Coulee Creek.

In the Kettle: Mary Ann Creek, Upper Myers Creek, Beaver Creek, Upper Toroda Creek, Cougar Creek.

In the Sanpoil: Cape Labelle Creek, Aeneas Creek, Lower Lost Creek, West Fork Granite Creek, Gold Creek.

In the Chief Joseph-Columbia: Upper Nespelem River, Lower Nespelem River, Upper Little Nespelem Creek, Mill Creek, Buffalo Lake, Hopkins Canyon, Tumwater Creek, Swamp Creek.

In the Okanogan: Aeneas Creek, Pine Creek, Upper Antoine Creek, Whisky Cache Creek, Tonasket Creek, Mosquito Creek, Coulee Creek, Hicks Canyon, Whitestone Creek, Lower Bonaparte Creek, Peony Creek, Lower Loup Loup Creek, Johnson Creek, Lower Omak Creek, Chewiliken Creek, Upper Tunk Creek, Soap Lake, Kartar Creek, McDonald Creek.

In the Methow: Black Canyon Creek, Gold Creek, Libby Creek, the Mainstem Lower Twisp River, War Creek, Davis Creek, Lower Beaver Creek, Bear Creek, Wolf Creek, Boulder Creek, Cub Creek, the Mainstem Lower Chewuch River, Eight Mile Creek, Wolf Creek, Early Winters Creek, Rattlesnake Creek, Goat Creek, the Lower Lost River.

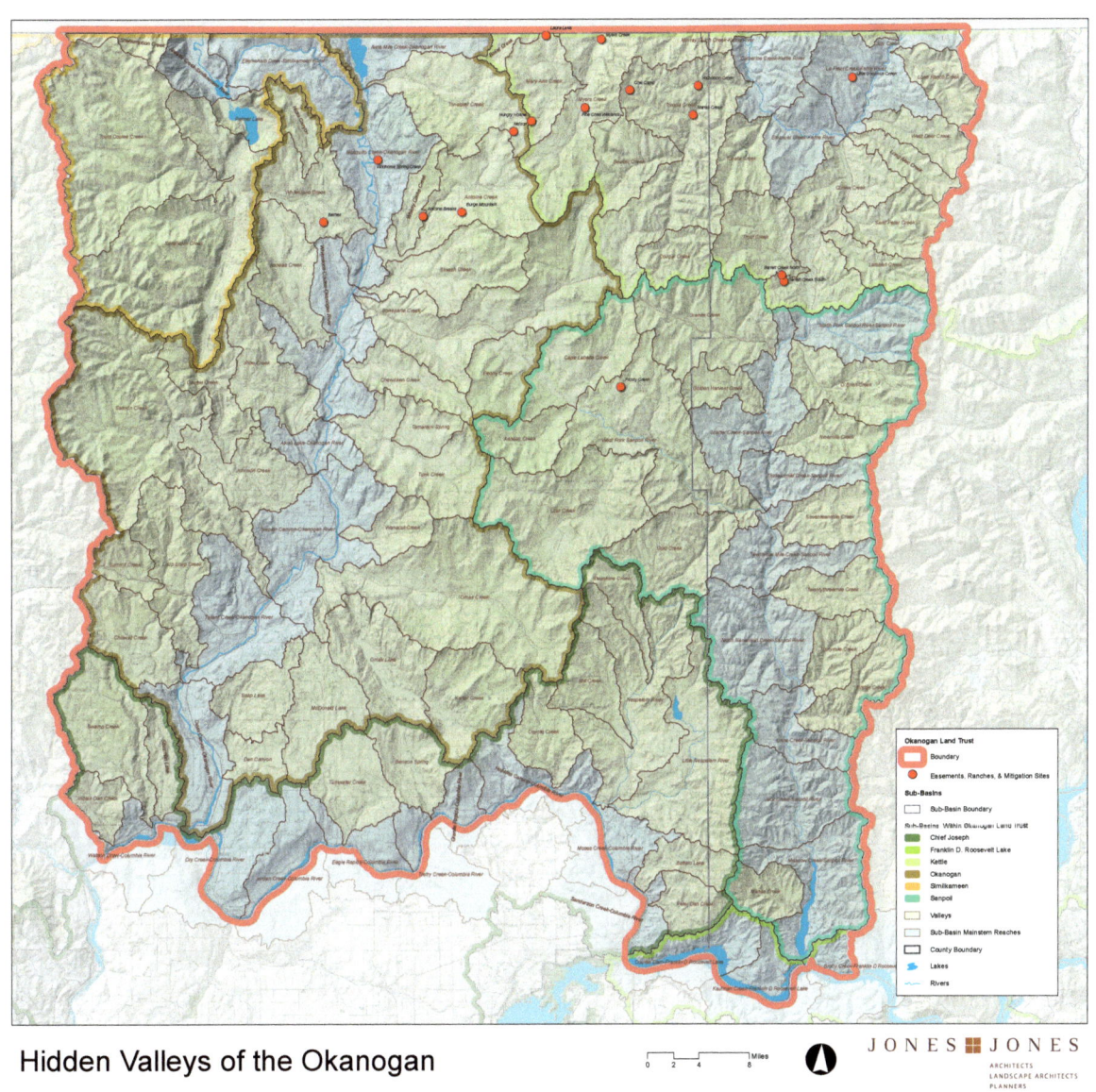

Hidden Valleys of the Okanogan

The Sandpoil　　　　Todd Thorn

www.ingramcontent.com/pod-product-compliance
Lightning Source LLC
Chambersburg PA
CBHW041957150426
43193CB00003B/40